Frost's Password System

Never forget another password!

Frost McKee

Frost's Password System
Never forget another password!

Frost McKee

Copyright Frost McKee 2012

Frost's Password System

Never forget another password!

Frost McKee

Passwords protect us from mayhem.

Would you want a stranger on your e-mail site? What sensitive information could they acquire there? You certainly wouldn't want them on your bank- site or social media site.

The problems with passwords are twofold:

1. You need a different password for every web site.
2. Remembering that many passwords can be very difficult.

There are several password storing programs that store all of your passwords digitally; all in one file. These files bring a smile to every hacker's face.

Frost's Password System

Never forget another password!

Frost McKee

Most people use the same two or three passwords for everything. They have probably used these for a long time. They are easily recalled because they mean something to them.

- Anniversary date
- A relative's or their own birthday
- Last four numbers of their social, driver's license, phone number
- Their license plate number
- Their favorite sports team
- Their favorite fruit, animal, plant
- A pet's name

These are easy to figure out and make

bad passwords.

Frost's Password System

Never forget another password!

Frost McKee

Just Imagine

- Having thousands of different passwords----
- All securely locked----
- Recalling them all with ease---

There are two attributes that every password needs:

- Memorability
    - The mnemonic part of the password
    - Adaptable for thousands of sites.
- Security
    - Unique Lock
    - One Great Personal Code (The main security of a password.)

Frost's Password System

Never forget another password!

Frost McKee

Memorability

How many times have you forgotten an important password? Well you're not alone. When I ask at the beginning of my seminar, what do you need help remembering? Passwords rate number three out of ten.

I have presented my memory training seminar, "Memorobics" for colleges, universities, fortune 500 companies and many others. I teach memory systems to help people remember names & faces, numbers, and school material.

I was listed in "The Guinness Book of World Records" for having memorized the random

Frost's Password System

Never forget another password!

Frost McKee

sequence of thirty-six decks of shuffled playing cards. (1,872)

When people hear about the listing, they naturally think I have a photographic memory. Nothing could be further from the truth. I have a trained memory. There were people who thought remembering that many playing cards would be impossible. It would be without a good mental system. To memorize the cards, I spent a little time designing a system, (a way of thinking) to accomplish the task. When I found myself forgetting passwords; I responded with a simple system to accomplish the task.

Frost's Password System

Never forget another password!

Frost McKee

The Basic System & the Personal Code

The Basic System is applied to each name of a site in the same sequence every time. This is your Mnemonic portion of your password. Apply the system the same way for each web-site and by looking at the site name, you will recall this portion of your password.

The Personal Code is a 4-6 character unique lock within your password. All of your passwords will be different and contain an impressive number of characters. It will work for thousands of sites and you only need to know two things in order to remember a limitless number of passwords.

The Basic System & Your Personal Code

Frost's Password System

Never forget another password!

Frost McKee

The Basic System

- Start with the first word in the web-site name.
- Find the first vowel in this word. (A, E, I, O, U)
- Use its numeric position in the alphabet (one, five, nine, fifteen, twenty-one) written out.
  See numerical alphabet (page 22)
- Find the last consonant (all letters that are not vowels) in this first word.
- Use its numeric position in the alphabet. Represented in numeric form. (12, 18, 22)
- Add your personal code to lock it up.

Frost's Password System

Never forget another password!

Frost McKee

Most people will find that The Basic System and a great Personal Code will more than meet their password needs. Some of you will want to do a little tweaking on the system.

The Basic System can be personalized to add even more security and give you a real feeling of ownership. There are thousands of ways to make it uniquely yours. Look at "Tweaking the Basic System" (page 23)

Frost's Password System

Never forget another password!

Frost McKee

The Personal code

A four to six character personal code will work for all of your web sites.

You want something totally unrelated to you. Something your best friend could never guess. This code will be used to secure every password.

When you are sure you have the code memorized, destroy any record of it. Never say it aloud and never write it. Store it only in your mind. (Not digitally). Tell no one.

Frost's Password System

Never forget another password!

Frost McKee

Good ideas for great personal codes

- A couple of words in a foreign language, you don't speak.
- The first letters of each word of a song title in your least favorite genre.
- The first letters of each word in a joke punch line. One you would never tell.
- A river and mountain range in a country where you have never been.
- Two foods you would never eat.
- An extinct animal and a planet.

You might consider a tweak in the Basic System for <u>very sensitive</u> sites. (pg.23)

- Banks
- E-mail
- Computer access
- Social network sites

Frost's Password System

Never forget another password!

Frost McKee

Examples:

The Basic Code with a Personal Code creating unique passwords.

Personal code = (egbdf)

EBay
five25egbdf

Netflix
five24egbdf

Craig's list
one19egbdf

Frost's Password System

Never forget another password!

Frost McKee

First National Bank
nine20egbdf

Social Security
fifteen12egbdf

Affordable Auto
one12egbdf

Frost's Password System

Never forget another password!

Frost McKee

Turkey Shoot
twenty-one25egbdf

Cloud Management
fifteen4egbdf

Mozilla Firefox
fifteen12egbdf

Frost's Password System

Never forget another password!

Frost McKee

Twitter
nine18egbdf

Merriam Webster
five13egbdf

A Blue Dog
one0egbdf

Note: A is the first word in "A Blue Dog" without a consonant. So the consonant would be zero.

Frost's Password System

Never forget another password!

Frost McKee

Try These Sites Yourself

- Use personal code egbdf.
- Remember: <u>never write your real code.</u>
- Check your answers on pages 19-21.

Corey's Bowling Lane

_____

John & Glen Self Storage

_____

Frost's Password System

Never forget another password!

Frost McKee

Amazon

_____

Fishing with Charlie

_____

Rowe Lane Elementary

_____

Frost's Password System

Never forget another password!

Frost McKee

YMCA

_____

Elmer's Convenience Store

_____

Adamo Real Estate

_____

Frost's Password System

Never forget another password!

Frost McKee

Correct password responses

Corey's Bowling Lane
fifteen19egbdf

John & Glen Self Storage
fifteen14egbdf

Frost's Password System
Never forget another password!

Frost McKee

Amazon
one14egbdf

Fishing with Charlie
nine7egbdf

Rowe Lane Elementary
fifteen23egbdf

Frost's Password System

Never forget another password!

Frost McKee

YMCA
one3egbdf

Elmer's Convenience Store
five19egbdf

Adamo Real Estate
one13egbdf

Frost's Password System
Never forget another password!
Frost McKee

Numerical Alphabet Sequence

A one	J 10	S 19
B 2	K 11	T 20
C 3	L 12	U twenty-one
D 4	M 13	
E five	N 14	V 22
F 6	O fifteen	W 23
G 7	P 16	X 24
H 8	Q 17	Y 25
I nine	R 18	Z 26

Tweaking the Basic System

"Make it yours"

("Amazon" examples with Personal code "egbdf")

1. <u>Start</u> with your personal code.
   egbdfone14

2. Enter your personal code between vowel and consonant.
   oneegbdf14

3. Add an extra 3 character personal code.
   - (*)one14egbdf
   - 372one14egbdf
   - ---one14egbdf
   - jfmone14egbdf

Frost's Password System

Never forget another password!

Frost McKee

4. Reverse vowel and consonant number representation.
   > 1fourteenegbdf

5. Move up or down the alphabet a predetermined number of letters.
   - up two on the vowel.
     three14egbdf
   - up two on the consonant.
     one16egbdf
   - down one on the consonant.
     one13egbdf

6. Add an extra number with the vowel.
   (*same number each time*) 8one14egbdf

Frost's Password System

Never forget another password!

Frost McKee

7. Try number 1. and 3. (above) together.
   egbdf+++one14

8. Try number 3. and 4. (above) together.
   1???fourteenegbdf

9. Try number 2. and 3. (above)together.
   ><*oneegbdf14

10. Try number 1. and 6. (above) together.
    egbdf8one14

Frost's Password System

Never forget another password!

Frost McKee

<u>Change your password on sensitive sites quarterly</u>.

- Banks
- E-mail
- Computer access
- Social network sites

I think you've got the idea now. You have seen the Basic system. You have some good ideas on how to pick a great personal code and you have seen several examples on tweaking the Basic System. Well, go out there, change all of your passwords to your new system, and feel confident you will never forget another password.

Thanks,

Frost McKee

Frost's Password System

Never forget another password!

Frost McKee

Notes

www.ingramcontent.com/pod-product-compliance
Lightning Source LLC
Chambersburg PA
CBHW061522180526
45171CB00001B/297